Robert Boodey Caverly

The Merrimac and its Incidents

Epic Poem

Robert Boodey Caverly

The Merrimac and its Incidents
Epic Poem

ISBN/EAN: 9783744652919

Printed in Europe, USA, Canada, Australia, Japan

Cover: Foto ©Thomas Meinert / pixelio.de

More available books at **www.hansebooks.com**

A Home in Centralville

THE MERRIMAC,

AND

ITS INCIDENTS.

AN EPIC POEM

BY
ROBERT B. CAVERLY.

BOSTON:
INNES & NILES, PRINTERS, 37 CORNHILL,
1865.

Entered, according to Act of Congress, in the year 1865, by
ROBERT B. CAVERLY,
In the Clerk's Office of the District Court for the District of Massachusetts

To the

REV. THEODORE EDSON, D. D.

FIRST RECTOR OF THE

FIRST CHURCH (ESTABLISHED IN 1824) IN LOWELL, "THE FIELD"

WHERE

ELLIOT,

IN 1674, PREACHED TO THE TRIBES OF

WONALANCET,

THIS VOLUME IS RESPECTFULLY DEDICATED.

CONTENTS.

	PAGE
The Creation	9
The Storm	10
The Torrent	11
The Landscape	8
The Sea	12
The Working of the Waters	13
Finny Tribes, First Appearance of	14
Animals, " " "	17
Birds, " " "	16
First Indian, Appearance of	17
The Indian's Habits and History	18
The Pilgrims coming, find *Squanto*, alias *Tisquantum*, "wandering here alone"	21

CONTENTS.

	PAGE
Samoset! his Personal Appearance, etc.	22
The First Treaty—Pilgrims with *King Massasoit*	23
Tisquantum dies, giving all this Domain to the Pilgrims	24
Progress in that Day	26
The Fifty Years' *Peace*, up to Philip's Time	26
Philip meditates War, and *Sassamon* divulges it to the Pilgrims	27
Sassamon is murdered by *Philip's* Men	27
The Murderers are tried in an English Court	27
Philip appears in Court, denying the Jurisdiction	27
Philip's Argument	28
The Murderers *Executed* is the first Step to *Philip's* War	29
The War, and *Philip's* Death	29
Peace	30
King William's War, and *Woman's* Heroism in that Day	33
The White Man's mode of Defence to Indian Warfare	34
The Story of the Capture of *Mrs. Dustin* and her two Assistants by the Indians;—the Slaughter of the Indians by them, and their final Escape from Captivity	35 to 49
Progress as made by the Pilgrims	50
The Revolution	51
The Veterans of the Revolution	51

CONTENTS.

	PAGE
Industry and Habits of the Generation next succeeding the Revolution, in the Seasons of	52
Haying	53
Threshing the Grain	54
Harvesting and Husking the Corn	55
The *Sabbath*-Day	57
Habits of the Household in the Olden Time	58
Modern Inventions	59
Progress in this Valley in the	
Building of Cities	60
Turning the River Power	60
Erecting Manufactories	60
Making Progress in Science as well as Art	61
The Railroad in this Valley, and its Work	62
The Telegraph and its Work	63
Improvements here in Husbandry	64
The SIX CITIES,— *Lowell, Manchester, Concord, Newburyport, Lawrence,* and *Nashua,* with the Villes and Towns on the MERRIMAC in their various Trades, Art, Science, and Industry	64 to 67

Of the many renowned Sons of this Valley, a few are named, to wit:

CONTENTS.

	PAGE
LOWELL and JACKSON, famed for Force of Character, and for Knowledge and Skill in the Arts	60
STARK and PIERCE, known to Revolutionary Fame	52
WEBSTER for Eloquence	67
PARSONS for Law and Learning	67
AYER for the extent of his operations in the Healing Art	65
WHITTIER for *truthful Song*	67
The Four Years' Rebellion; and the rush from this Valley to resist it	68
The Force employed in its Overthrow	69
LINCOLN, GRANT, SHERMAN, and SHERIDAN	71, 72
TISQUANTUM'S Return to the MERRIMAC	73

THE MERRIMAC.

CELESTIAL Bards! in magic numbers skilled
We thee invoke; *who*, blest with music *filled*,
Chant high in heaven above, yet present *here*,
Deign oft to witness in this earthly sphere
What mortals do, and what of good or ill
In truthful song is celebrated still,
And what of beauty grand in Nature lives,
What Heaven ordains and what experience gives,
Yet left unsung, — *inspired attend*, repair
Up to yon mountain-top, in regions fair,
Where prospect wide above the woodland shade
Unfolds the works creative wisdom made, —

THE MERRIMAC.

Survey proud Merrimac,[1] whose praise we sing,
And to mine aid some grateful measure bring, —
Some note of landscape grand in dale and hill,
Adorned with glittering lake, cascade, or rill,
With forest wild, with winding wave between
The giant groves along the valley green;
Fair floral regions sweet at early dawn,
And fields of lilies in the dewy lawn, —
Whate'er thy vision meets, o'er all the plain,
From mountain height to ocean's wide domain,
Of rural Nature or of handy Art,
In truthful numbers faithfully impart.
Nor *sights* alone observe, but *sound*, of birds,
The lambkin-bleatings, and the lowing herds,
The cuckoo's echo at the close of day,
And wakeful whippoorwill's wild warbling lay,
That cheer the vale; — with chime of village bell,
Which wakes, to thought divine, *Pilgrims* that dwell

THE MERRIMAC.

Along the broad highway,—whose voices swell
Praises to *Him* who "doeth all things well;"—

With these and more, our humble song indite,
That tend to raise the soul by Nature's light
To light of *Heaven*, and to the fruitful source
Whence all things came to pass and took their
    course.

Sweet river! *thy true source,* which angels sung
At the *creation* when the world begun,
We *seek;* and how thy rills of *chaos, born,*
First leaped, rejoicing in their native form;—
When bleak New England's height began to rise,
And moon and stars just formed lit up the skies;
How the Great God on high, with outstretched
    hand,
Divided waters from the massive land,

THE MERRIMAC.

Scooped the vast concave of the ocean bed,
And infant channels for the rivers made;
And how and when his wisdom next arranges
To move the stagnant floods by natural changes,
Compel the seas their rugged bounds forsake,
Becloud the hills, and shining rivers make;
To make thin vapors, heated to excess,
On ocean *more*, on terra-firma less,
Out from the briny waves incessant rise
Above the hills, and back to other skies,
Combine in clouds, and vast collections form,
Spreading the heavens with impending storm.
Whence earth itself full formed begins to move
Through mighty conflicts by the hand of Jove
Outward and *onward* from its native source
Round with the whirling spheres to take its course.

Now then the forkèd light, ascending high,

THE MERRIMAC.

Unveils the *terrors* of a *troubled* sky;
Tempestuous gales in darkness intervene,
Sweeping the *world* with *howlings* in *extreme*
And *thunderings loud;* the clouds, let loose in drops,
Dash down their *showers* on the mountain-tops.

   Then leap the streamlets from the mountain-waste
As if by stern command requiring haste,
As if *God's* power with screw and lever *plied*,
Squeezing the lofty hills to raise the tide,
Would drown the earth in awful floods sublime,
For local sin, or want of faith divine,
As since in wrath he did in Noah's time.

   Thus at creation's dawn did Merrimac
Begin to flow. The storm subsides, and *light*,
Bright gleaming sunbeams, broke from sable night.

THE MERRIMAC.

And now the Sweeping Wave, with banks o'erflown,
Brilliant and *grand*, 'mid azure splendor *shone*,
Rolls on, — and with accumulated force
Of mighty waters on their destined course
Through naked banks, ne'er washed by waves
    before, —
Now *curving* o'er the cliff with dashing roar
Of cataract; now *swelling* far and wide
Down sloping vales in full majestic tide;
Then *gliding* smooth, as plain or meads ensue,
In tranquil pride resplendent bravely through,
Conveys her fountains to the untried shore
Where *wave* or flood, had never reached before, —

    To form a *sea*, and on the world bestow
A vast highway, with tides to ebb and flow;
In light refulgent, in extent sublime,
To swarm with joyous life through endless time,

THE MERRIMAC.

To float huge ships in commerce and in strife,
Of unborn nations, waking into life.
Through constant heat her atoms rise again
Floating in transit backward whence they came,
Feeding the stream with purer founts anew,
Which, made *eternal*, onward still pursue;
Both flood and vapor in one circuit run,
Like planet in her orb about the sun,
Or, like the life-blood coursing through the vein
By means of arteries return again,
Sustaining man's frail body from his birth,—
So moving waters do the vital earth;
Pervading Nature's germs and fibres free,
Upward in channels creep through herb and tree,
They deck the daisy in her checkered bloom,
And swell the rose to yield a sweet perfume,
Are felt in trunk, in branch, in bud and leaves,
And thence escape in clouds, borne on the breeze;—

THE MERRIMAC.

Emblem of the "*Eternal!*" in their round
E'er free to give, but ne'er exhausted, found.

Next near the shore now gliding glittering seen,
Minnows innumerous in the waters green,
Minute in size, some faster fuller grown,
Each for an end, yet then unseen, unknown,
In caves now playful cautious prone to be,
Then out in depth of waters sporting free,
Each draws from Heaven the fleeting breath of life,
Here to subsist through elemental strife,
Varied in species, color, and in form,
Some cold in temperament, others warm,
Each to its kind attached, prolific, free
To seek and share a common destiny.
In lapse of time, from tiny minim grown,
The *whale* loomed up in vast proportion shown,—
Now restless seeks more spacious depths to gain,

THE MERRIMAC.

And finds a homestead in the briny main.
Huge sturgeons, too, — all fish of larger growth, —
Swelled the deep current *seaward splashing* forth;
While smaller forms, as trout and pickerel,
Inhabit *native* stream, content to dwell
Fresh-water tenants, tranquil quite as yet,
By foe unsought, unhurt by hook or net.

While *others* rove. The favorite salmon tries
The Arctic seas, in light of other skies;
Yet oft as spring betides the Merrimac,
His out-bound path he fondly follows back
With finny tribes. Then through the inlets trace
A countless progeny, an infant race
From hidden spawns, to swarm the harmless shore,
Then gambol outward, onward, as before,
Quiet, yet quick in transit to and fro,
E'er keen to *see*, what makes for weal or woe,

THE MERRIMAC.

They drink sweet joys in light of nature given,
And fill a purpose grand, ordained of Heaven.

    Meanwhile the tree for fruit and forest, sprung
From latent life beneath the soil, begun
To spread in varied shadows mother earth,
Verdant and fruitful; in productive birth,
Alike of *insects* strange, of *beast* or bird,
In *pairs* connubial, fit for flock or herd.
As thus 'mid thicket dense, or bower green,
In earth or air, at first half hidden seen,
The merest mites; — thence formed and fluttering move,
Unfeathered owls, the raven, hawk, and dove; —
Whence flaunts the eagle due in course of time,
And songsters, warbling, wing for every clime.
Whence all the nervy tenants of the air,
From proudest swan to flitting insect rare;

THE MERRIMAC.

Whence clods of earth and drops of water pure,
First fraught with life, with life can but endure.

Of tardy growth sleek whelps in tiny form,
From latent caverns in the hill-side warm,
Of *lion* race, and beasts of other kind,
At length emerge and habits varied find.

Then next from curious germ beneath the sod,
Now blest in needful care of Nature's God,
Whose eye all-seeing here began to scan
The strange invention of *mysterious man*,—
By vigorous thrift, as fell the beaming rays
Of Phœbus, fitly felt on vernal days,
Came forth an *Indian's** infant form divine,

---

* The natives were called Indians by Columbus through mistake, who at first supposed he had arrived on the eastern shore of India, by which error they took their name.

THE MERRIMAC.

First spawn of manhood on the stream of time;
Basking in valleys wild, earth-formed, earth-fed
For ripened age, — by native reason led,
And chief o'er beast and bird in power became
A fitful terror to the timid game.

Increased at length by nature's self-same laws
To numerous tribes prolific, men and squaws,
From artful wigwams new, spread o'er the land,
First skill evinced in architecture grand,
He wanders wild, belted with arrows keen,
And blest with knowledge right and wrong between,
A stately Priest at peace. Provoked to *strife*,
He wields a hatchet and a scalping-knife
With dire revenge. E'er true to self and squaw
He knows no faith, no code, but Nature's law.
His footsteps fondly dwell where now we trace
Primeval heirlooms of the human race;

THE MERRIMAC.

The chisel smooth and tomahawk first made
Of stone, ere Art had formed the iron blade;
Where, from a narrow dock with native crew,
He launched, in naval pride, the first canoe
And ploughed the Merrimac. His dripping oar
Ripples the waters never pressed before, —
Bestirs the scaly tribes to nervous fear
For rights most sacred thus invaded here.
As if by instinct they the chieftain knew
To be a tyrant and a glutton too,
Intent on native beast, on bird or fish,
By slaughter dire to fill a dainty dish;
Whose *webs* are *nets* from bark of trees alone,
And *mills that grind* are mortars made of stone;
Who clothed his tribes, if clad they e'er appear,
In raiment plundered from the bounding deer;
Who maketh treacherous hooks from guiltless bones,
And drags a deadly net o'er sacred homes.

THE MERRIMAC.

And *thus*, o'er land and stream for ages long,
A race of red men, vagrant, plod along,
With language, taught from rustic Nature's throne,
And habits, each peculiarly their own;
On growth spontaneous fed, content with prey,
What serves the purpose of a single day.
Their God is seen afar at rise of sun;
Their life in heaven is hunting here begun;
By laws unwritten, Sachems rule the tribes,
And lead the host, wherever ill betides,
To fatal war. By force of arrows, hurled,
They reigned sole monarchs in this western world.

The countless years thus passed of man's career,
Fraught with achievements oft enacted here;
With works of skill, what human thought could
    do;
With grand exploits, or deeds of direful hue;

THE MERRIMAC.

With kings and prophets, chief in note or worth,
Through generations vast, transpired on earth,
Make but a blank in time's historic lore,
Till voyagers from another world came o'er;—
Columbus first of all; then many more
Within a hundred years, then next, before
The Pilgrims land,[3]— adventurers indeed,—
From Adam sprung, juniors in *race* and *breed*,
But versed in letters, statute law, and art,
Seniors in science, just in head and heart.

They meet old SQUANTO wandering here alone,
Who, sore depressed, bereaved of friends and home,
Recounts events which true tradition brought,
Of Indian life, what sad experience taught,
How, far and near, the dead unburied lay,
His own Patuxet tribes all swept away;
Yet nations seaward, deep in woods afar,

Spared from the scourge of pestilence and war,
Still thrive. There Massasoit, whose power maintains
The peace of tribes, in full dominion reigns.

 From thence SAMOSET comes, with heart and hand,
To "welcome Englishmen" and grant them land;
His visage dark with long and raven hair,—
No treacherous marks his beardless features bear;
With frame erect and strangely painted o'er,
Belted around his loins, a Sagamore,
Whose bony arm a bow and arrow held,
A heart unsoiled his tawny bosom swelled
To generous deeds. He broken English spake,
And talked anon of men,—of Francis Drake,[2]
That gallant white man, years before who came,
And gave New Albion her historic name,—

Of Captain Smith who since surveyed the coast,
And other voyagers, now a scattered host, —
Of former days some history tried to give,
And "lay of land" where rambling red men live.
Truthful SAMOSET proves, and seeks to bring
The Pilgrim saints in audience with his king.

Then Massasoit, the king, and chiefs appear;
As well the governor and suit draw near,
By music led, and soldiers at command,
Clad in the homespun of a foreign land,
And greet the king. The *king* no armor bears,
Save on his breast a knifelike weapon wears,
White beads about his neck, a gaudy ring,
And quaint tobacco bag, suspended by a string,
Comprise the insignia of his regal power,
Known and observed of nations as of yore.

THE MERRIMAC.

Both king and chiefs, with painted features, *wear*
Feathers disjoined from birds of plumage rare,
But little else. Kindly in turn they greet [4]
The Pilgrim band, and down in group now seat
Themselves, holding discourse of allied strength
In treaty,[5] and, when all agreed, at length,
They pass the pipe around, each *drink*[6] in turn.
A sacred compact thus they all confirm,—
A treaty wise, that full contentment gives
For fifty years while Massasoit lives.

Squanto meanwhile who'd served a peaceful end,
And in the Pilgrims' God had found a Friend,
Bereaved and worn by care of bygone years
In mazy pathways through a vale of tears,
Falls sick; and as by fever low depressed,
And life in doubt, to Pilgrims thus addressed

THE MERRIMAC.

His sovereign will: "This hunting-ground is mine;
The lakes, the vales, those mountain heights sublime,
The green-grown banks where Merrimac bright glows
And all the *hills* far as Pawtucket goes,—
These *spacious wilds*, my kindred, now no more,
In full dominion held, and hunted o'er;
Then dying, all their titles thence descend
To me, TISQUANTUM,[7] now so near this end
Of life. To thee, my Pilgrim Friends, I *give*
This broad domain; here may the white man
      live;—
My bow and arrow, too,—I give thee all.
Hence let me go, obedient to the call
Of angel Death. Adieu!"
                      Thus gracious dies
The last red *man* beneath Patuxet skies,
And thus the English sole possession share,
By will from SQUANTO, all this region fair,

THE MERRIMAC.

Forever thence, to lay the forest low,
To fence fair fields, and drive the crooked plough,
To waste the wigwams which for ages spread
The wild, and build broad mansions in their stead;
Schoolhouses, temples to the GOD of grace,
And cities proud, peculiar to the race
Of *Adam*. Diligent through honest toil,
They reap rich harvest from the virgin soil.
From culture urged with bold, aggressive sway,
Wild beasts, becoming frantic, flee away.
As ravenous bears and moose and wolves recede
Black-cat-tle and the noble horse succeed
In aid of husbandry.* Full flocks abound;
The herds increase as roll the seasons round;
The desert e'en, through culture's grateful care,
Soon set with fruit, begins to bloom and bear;
Fair Nature smiles responsive to the plan
Of faith in God and industry of man.

THE MERRIMAC.

Next follows war. Dread anarchy appears,
As if to blast the crowning thrift of years
At death of MASSASOIT. Philip succeeds
As king,⁸ and hostile to the whites proceeds
To flagrant deeds; and first of all in time,
A native priest,* suspected of no crime
But to have broached a secret plot, is slain ¹⁰
By murderous hand. On Philip rests this stain
Of blood; and Justice stern but waits to draw
Her penal sword by force of English law
Against the natives. 'Tis not long withheld;
By strong indictment seized, arraigned, and held,
Tobias and confederates are tried
By petit-jury, white and red allied,
Whose doubtful jurisdiction Philip pleads,
And to address the Forum thus proceeds:—

* John Sassamon.

THE MERRIMAC.

"What right, what law, these prisoners to arraign
Have Englishmen in this my own domain?
What lease of venue from allotted lines
To make invasion and adjudge of crimes?
Why seek the Indian's life in guile forlorn —
Of these three men of native mothers born;
Who, one and all, with SASSAMON, the slain,
Were my liege subjects, bound by *laws* the same
Which governed tribes a thousand years ago,
But which evaded brings an endless woe?
What mind, what project, prompts your boundless sway
But hence to drive the red man far away
From this fair land, his birthright and his wealth,
And hold these regions vast through royal stealth?
With flagrant wrong the tribes will ne'er concur,
And to your bold intrusion I demur!

THE MERRIMAC.

My subjects here an English court may try;
By spurious judgments, they may fall and die;
Yet vengeance dread shall point the red man's steel,
And to the God of battles I'll appeal."

Philip withdrew, and ne'er returned again;
His truthful talk was uttered but in vain.
The prisoners held and thus condemned to die
Brought darkness gathering o'er the western sky.
"The bloody sunset" and the forkèd light
That broke the curtain of that fearful night,
Awaking English matrons, 'mid alarms,
To hug sweet infants with tenacious arms,
Foretold gross carnage of successive years
And devastation in a land of tears.

True to his word, which prudence thus defied,
Philip the Pilgrims fought, and, fighting, died,"

THE MERRIMAC.

With countless victims by the self-same blade,
Which mutual madness had in folly made.

And which in blood by oft-recurring strife
Through conflicts desperate kindled into life
By hate implacable still lingering long
Avenges Philip's death, and flagrant wrong
Remembered well, *encroachments rash, designed,*
Repeated oft, as self had long inclined
The strangers here. But through the lapse of time,
Whence wayward hearts to better faith incline,
Whence discord wanes away,— then *truth* began
To shed with light the vagrant paths of man;
Distracted foes their errors soon discern,
And back to reason once again return.

Then *Peace,* that welcome harbinger of health,
Of generous thrift, foreshadowing weal and wealth,

THE MERRIMAC.

Brings her glad tidings down and cheers the land,
With prompt good-will, and noble deeds at hand,
To heal the broken heart, to make amends
For wilful waste, which from the past descends.

   Thence this fair vale from mountain to the main
In vernal grandeur buds to bloom again,
And plenteous harvest with her golden ears
Crowning the prudence of progressive years
Adorns the field, and grace triumphant gives
To honest toil. Here WONALANCET[12] lives
Unscathed by war, a sachem wise and true,—
Of fragment tribes still roving far and few
Along these banks where PENNAKOOK[13] had stood
For countless years, through tempest, storm, and
      flood;—
And further seaward where WAMESIT[14] lies,
Still well intrenched, a wigwam city thrives,

THE MERRIMAC.

Rightly reserved the home of hunters here,
A fort within, and habitations dear
To friendly red men. While from dearth released,
From scourge of conflict and in strength increased,
Through many a favored year the *Pilgrim mind*,
By faith and works, religious freedom find;
Such as the *Fathers* sought and had foretold
Should come, in grace abounding as of old.

At length the *French* with *England* disagree,
Which next portends what carnage hence shall be,
What man's estate must prove,—a varied life;—
From *quiet peace* proceeds terrific *strife;*
From plenty, *dearth;* from faith and virtue, *sin;*
From health, *disease*, that wages war within.

Thus strangely intermixed are good and ill;
True to the purpose of a sovereign will

THE MERRIMAC.

Nature but thrives by fire that burns within,
From planets *broken*, other worlds begin.
Yet bloody conflicts, *such* the world abhor
As mark the advent of avenging war;
And such the crime that now involves the race,
Fraught with its cruel curse and deep disgrace,
That through successive years again devours
The vital substance of contending powers.

From war-whoops wild, and earth in crimson
    glow,
A wail goes up, — a note of *woman's* woe!
Fierce vengeance tempts her *singleness* of heart,
Her *heroism true*, her *guileless art*,
Her *purity*, her own *maternal care*,
Her *faith* in God, that never knows despair,
Her *love* indeed, that triumphs most and best
In *trial sad*, when most by danger pressed;

THE MERRIMAC.

Whose *truth endures,* when fails our vital breath,
Inspires fond hope, and smooths the bed of death.

   Such were the hearts whose wails went up afar,
That brooked the fury of King William's War;[18]
Whose just protection, savages defied,
And dearest hopes of house and home denied;
Around her hearth from hidden ambush springs
The lurking foe, and death, with horror, brings.

   And this is war! — and such in wrath makes haste
To lay the white man's cot and village waste;
That deals in *daggers* poisoned, — *coated* o'er, —
The fagot torch, and gluts on human gore.

   Against such crime the settlers strong unite;

THE MERRIMAC.

In various ways they rally for the fight;
Some seek defence by force of gun and dogs;
Some take to *garrisons*, strong built of logs,
And some in squads with weapons *rude* assail
The *foe*, and fierce pursue the hidden trail.
'Twas so at NEWBURY and at BRADFORD TOWN,
Far further north and seaward further down,
Along the vale where'er the white man dwelt,
Still unprovoked the selfsame scourge was felt.

And at old HAVERHILL, as "MATHER"[18] tells,
The flaring fagot burns where DUSTIN dwells.
That faithful father, frenzied to dismay,
Hastens the flight of children far away,
But not the infant; *that* in wrath is slain.
Its *mother*, captured, trudges in the train
Of savages; while in the clouds are shown
The crackling ruins of an *English* home.

THE MERRIMAC.

The tribes evade pursuit; they skirt the glen,
Fast hastening through the fields away, and *then*
Dense woods and sable night conceal the foe; —
There, couched on broken boughs in beds of snow,
Repose they seek. Still mindful of the past,
Her heart depressed, by sleep benumbed at last,
There dreams *that mother*, weary, sick, at rest,
Of happy *home*, — of father, children blest, —
Of life's sweet joys profusely, kindly given, —
Of angel visits from the throne of Heaven, —
Of that true bliss religious life inspires,
That wafts the soul above earth's frail desires, —

    Thus moved congenial thought her dreamy
        mind
As moved that mighty forest in the wind, —
Thus, on, — till twilight gray with breaking beam
Now *turns* the *tenor* of a fleeting dream;

THE MERRIMAC.

When half aroused, before her vision *gaze*
Appear *grim visages* and fagot blaze; —
Tall spectres, gaunt, whose garments drip with gore
From that infanticide the day before,
Wrought strange convulsions. Whence that fearful wail?
'Twas Hannah Dustin," waking for the trail.

Her dark brown hair back on her shoulders spread,
The frosts of night still on her garments laid.
At sight of death, at sound of war-whoop cry,
Avenging justice flashes in her eye;
Still, far beyond the cloud-capt *tree-tops*, shown,
There gleamed in prospect *yet* another home;
Light paints a *tinge* upon her pallid brow,
And up to God above she made a vow;
For on the *trees* are marks of kindred blood,

THE MERRIMAC.

And vengeance just is whispered in the wood.
Firm as the granite *hills that brave* the storm,
That mother's *will* is *fixed*, and waxes warm.
Yet held to follow through the rugged way,
Kept equal step for many a weary day
('Twas death to falter 'mid a savage throng)
With Mary Neff[18] and boy,[19] all move along
Through winding paths and tangled wildwood fens,
Where prowled the wolf, and where the serpent dens,
Declivities they wind, and ford the brooks
That leap the mountain pass from granite rocks;
Thence in dark thicket, then in sunlight gleam,
And then in boats of *birch* on spacious stream,
Up where old Contoocook unites in pride
With *Merrimac*, profound in rolling tide;
There, on an island *wild*, are captives shown
The wigwam rude, an Indian's favored home.

THE MERRIMAC.

And there on mats, around the camp-fire flame,
Seated in group, they glut the slaughtered game,
Which hunger sought; and night, now gathering in,
Spreads her dark mantle o'er the woods within;
While from afar, a gentle zephyr breeze
Plays grateful music on the waving trees,
Inviting *rest* from th' rambling drudge of day,
That lulls the spirit from the world away.

Still does that zephyr omens strange portend,
A baleful bickering, some tragic end;
Yet ne'er more safe, ne'er less by danger pressed,
Than felt the drowsy foe reclined at rest;—
And *sleep sonorous*, which fatigue inspires,
Drowns deep the tribe in front of midnight fires.

Then rose that mother, noiseless, moving near
To Neff, breathes mandates startling to her ear;

THE MERRIMAC.

To Samuel, too, her vent of vengeance went
That fired his heart. They move with joint intent
And signal stealth. Around the foe they felt,
And drew a tomahawk *each*, from the belt,
That touched his loins; and then erect they stand
Lifting that bloody blade with heedful hand; —
Down on his guilty head, three times they strike,
And *three* times *three* DEATH follows, each alike.

No groan nor sigh is heard, nor sign of woe;
But stiff and cold there lies the bloody foe
'Neath clouds of night; the wigwam embers fade, —
And phantom-shadows stalk along the glade
In depth of woods. The hills are hushed aloof, —
No voice, save from the owl or hungry wolf,
That clamors for his prey.

      Yet as these three,
Once captive bound, now turn away, *thus free*,

THE MERRIMAC.

Bright beaming stars, through parted clouds between,
True guides intent from Heaven's arch serene,
Look down; while *truth*, still valiant to prevail
O'er wrong, and justice stern with even scale,
Approve the deed; and from that crimson glade,
That dark, lone wigwam with unburied dead,
Relieved, yet sad, they board a light canoe
To dip the oar in hope of home, pursue
Adown bright Merrimac in generous tide,
That bears the craft on high through borders wide,—
Thence paddling *east*, they gain a favored shore
Above the fall, where troubled waters roar
Below,—all safe at land.
               The day-star rose,
Nature anon awakes from night's repose,
Wild birds from far thick gathered in the trees

THE MERRIMAC.

Warble sweet welcome on the morning breeze
To strange adventurers; while all that day
Along the winding shore that leads the way
To Haverhill, they thoughtful trudge and talk,
What each had seen in life's bewildered walk, —
Of childhood years beguiled with favorite toys, —
Of love, — of home delights, — of buried joys.

   Thus did the women mutual converse hold,
Till Samuel from mutest manner cold
Bespoke them thus. "What mean these signs of pain?
These crimson marks that through my garments stain?
Did such from veins of Bampaco descend,
Who gave me bow and arrow as a friend?
Truth undisguised these morning beams disclose,
The sure avenger of his dying woes!

THE MERRIMAC.

Unwelcome tints! they haunt my homeward way
And at the threshold threatened to betray
Me there. Shall I, long-lost, a mother's boy,
Return and *pangs impart* instead of joy
To such a heart? No,—leave me here; unknown
To seek some hidden cave aloof from home;
Or send me, captive bound, to dwell again
In tents, afar from her who mourns me slain,—
Whence crime concealed shall never vent a stain
Nor rumor sad to blot a cherished name."

He said, and there half halting stood
Till Mary chides him in a different mood;—

"I pray thee, Samuel, list to me awhile,—
Misgivings sad attend but to beguile
Thy youth. But list,—they move me to descry
In wrong, if thou art guilty, so am I;

THE MERRIMAC.

For at the war-whoop cry I could have fled,
And shunned captivity, its horrors dread;
Yet would not yield to fate that infant dear,
Nor fail my mistress kind through selfish fear.
Alarmed, I seized it from the cradle there; —
That life, I begged a furied fiend to spare
At risk of self. Yet we no favor gain;
Our plea, our prayers most fervent, all in vain!
Impelled, from horrors which this heart had stung,
To our liege mother and to thee I clung,
In bonds a comrade held, a volunteer
In all the dangers dread of such career.
I've more to fear than thou, who, found alone,
Wert forced at Worcester from parental home
By brutal foes. Grim cruelties they sought,
But on themselves relentless vengeance brought,
In which an agent I indeed was one
To bear a part in wrong, if wrong were done —

THE MERRIMAC.

If in the shed of blood a crime it be,
To break from hell-born bondage to be free,
Then is the fault in me much more than thee,
Who had no choice of lot nor chance to flee.
Yet have I faith from inward teachings given,
Life's freedom gained is justified of Heaven;
Whose care paternal henceforth let us trust,
As did our fathers, faithful from the first."

Thus did they talk of self, of wrong and right,
Meandering along till late at night
Through narrow pathways, hindered now and then
By tangled thicket dark, by brook and fen.
Then next by range of hills, where lies at length
A deep ravine, and there, through lack of strength,
They turn aside beneath a shelving rock
O'ergrown of spreading pines; thither to stop,
Inclined to rest; but fain would *wakeful* keep,

Yet, lost anon by force of needful sleep,
Remain still there, till morn's refulgent ray
Reflected on the wave of Nashua,[20]
Cast varied shadows in the branchy wood
Around the group.

                    There "mother Dustin" stood
Invoking favors from the throne of God
To be bestowed in coming time for good
For Mary Neff, for Samuel the same,
Her pilgrim comrades, whence deliverance came—

And briefly now, as ended then her prayer,
Addressed them each in turn still waiting there
In kindness thus: "Mary, to thee I owe
Much more of *debt* than I can e'er bestow
Of earth's reward. Thy truthfulness of heart,
Thy generous constancy, thy guileless art,
In trial proved, this thankful soul reveres;

THE MERRIMAC.

May blessings, Mary, crown thy future years;
My home is thine, if home I see again,
Devoutly favored thou shalt there remain.

"And you, dear Samuel, *valiant* in the past,
Honest in purpose, faithful to the last,
No more should doubt. To savages belong
The retribution of relentless wrong,
And not to thee. Are not His dealings just
Who Israel led? Shall we our God distrust?
No. — Brood no more of doubts, most noble boy!
Go, seek thy way to Worcester; bear true joy
To her who bore thee, and whose hallowed care
Shall haste thee onward to her presence there,
Still *undisguised*, in *truth* of *God* still led,
Wash *not a stain* from out thy garments red.
Thy deeds but known shall welcome truth impart;
They'll prove the valor of a valiant heart.

THE MERRIMAC.

Take yonder *skiff;* 'twill be no trespass done,
For thee it *drifted* from a fate unknown.
For thee my voice in thanks shall hence ascend;
Away! and blessings on thy life attend."

Still loath to part, yet harboring doubts no more,
The lad, wide wafted on the westward shore,
His beckoning paddle raised; with aprons, too,
The women, answering, waved their last adieu.

Thence turning, — tearful, meditating mild
On distant "*dear ones,*" wandered through the wild,
And Haverhill reached: — to whom, from governors even,
Came generous gifts and thankful plaudits given.

And there they rest. There upward points, to-day,

THE MERRIMAC.

A monument of stone from Dustin's clay.
Her noble deeds are held in high renown,
Sacred like *heirloom* in that ancient town;
And long as Merrimac's bright waters glide
Shall stand that mother's *fame*, still by its side.

Such were the bickerings that brought the woes
Of *William's* time; which from the tribes arose
Through sordid hate, that rankled in the place
Of gospel *truth*, unknown to such a race.

Enough of war. Yet others still there were
Profuse in blood. 'Tis man's estate to err.
Let pass *Queen Anne's*,[21] the troubles of her day,
The craft of Jesuits, fruitful of dismay;
Nor need to note the *French and Indian*[22] strife,
Nor trace the torch, the tomahawk, and knife
Further. 'Tis now the olive-branch divine,

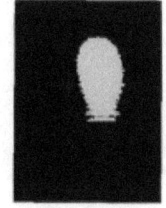

THE MERRIMAC.

That springs from culture's agency benign,
With better deeds the record to embalm,
Succeeds the war of Wolf against Montcalm.

Now industry with thrift again moves on,
Blest in the fruits of earth and arts anon,
While Science fair her grateful tribute brings,
And Charity, with healing in her wings,
To faith and works. The colonies incline
To independence, and in strength combine;
The tribes remote from civil life retire,
Still wandering wild as wont through frail desire,
Leave free the field to prosper many a year
Unstained of war, in fruitful bounties fair.

Then self-control begins to seek solution,
A thirst for freedom threatens revolution.
At first provoked by Britain's indiscretion,

THE MERRIMAC.

Her power assumed, her flagrant legislation,
And other wrongs, invasion comes at length,
Resistance follows, — then a tug at strength
Full seven years.[23] On hostile fields, engaged,
The armies gathered, and the battle raged.

John Bull, in strength of scientific drill,
Inflamed the ardor of untutored skill; —
The Yankee's fire-lock belched terrific flame,
Against whose vengeance science was but vain; —
And scythe and pitchfork wielded for the right
The better weapons proved, in such a fight.
True *valor* thus from pilgrim hearts of yore,
Drove the brave Britons from Columbia's shore.

Then through the vale, the *Veteran* we trace,
Firm in deportment, faithful to his race,
Down from the fields of conquest and renown,

Observed of all the host, the heroes of the town; —
BEN. PIERCE[24] is there far seen amid the throng,
With laurels crowned, they wind the way along; —
And there's old JOHN[25] who, when the field was dark,
Would risk his life at risk of *"Molly Stark."*
These were our fathers, manly in their might
From whom descended liberty and right.

Where now they rest shall fragrant flowers grow;
Their valiant deeds shall coming ages know;
And filial care shall cherish evermore,
That noble tree they planted at our door.

So wasteful revolution passed away
Like *darkest hour*, foreshadowing brilliant day.

Now smiling spring comes in from winter's blast
To swell the seed; and now the bloom is past;

THE MERRIMAC.

Productive seasons flit their hours away,
Each warms the world in bounty day by day,
That living things in nature may survive,
That man and beast that come and go may thrive.
From varied gifts subsistence we devise,
And in due season gather in supplies.
The husbandman hath care for weighty sheaves,
Yet for a time unthreshed the grain he leaves;
While down the meadow, *mowers* all the way
Swing swath on swath of verdant heavy hay, —
Tagged there by Johnny, *tossing* it in air,
To make the *crop* while yet the field is fair;
The rakers next, — the teamster in his turn,
With rugged cart and oxen, comes anon,
Each vies in *strength*, in manly *ardor* shown,
To *glean* the *glen*, and *bear* the harvest home.
But when dark clouds thick gather o'er the sky,
They quit the fumid field to thresh the rye,

THE MERRIMAC.

Up to the barn, a grandsire *built* of old,
Where frightened swallows weary wings unfold
Above. There face to face within the door,
In squads divided on the spacious floor; —
The heavy sheaves lay head to head between,
The swinging flails *high* in the air are seen,
Blow follows blow, and strength to strength they vie,
The bundles *bounding* rattle out the rye.

As when two *charioteers* by Bacchus strong
Inflamed, now homeward lash their steeds *along*
O'er yonder bridge, — swift whirl the wheels
    around
By dint of trial, — and heavy hoofs *rebound*.
So from the floor the farmer's noisy flail
Reverberates aloud along the vale, —

Then *note*, when evening gathers o'er the plain,

THE MERRIMAC.

Now laid at length a heavy heap of *grain;*
There to be winnowed, when old Boreas blows,
Then high the chaff in cloudy current flows,
And from the lifted measure *shaken* seen,
The grain in conic pile falls pure and clean;
Then stored in bin, or cask, safe-held at will,
Awaits the money-market or the mill.

 Meanwhile the field assumes a spiky form;
The time hath come to gather in the corn;
On hand the laborers, on hand the cart,
The lads are all aglee to take a part;
For *now they know* when eve approaches near,
'Twill bring that joyful *husking* of the year.
All now one purpose faithfully fulfil,
The rustling ears are hurried from the hill
With ardent zeal; and flushed with hopeful joys
Above the standing stocks both men and boys

THE MERRIMAC.

High on their shoulders *crowded baskets wield*.
The heavy harvest carted from the field,
They pile in heaps within the grating door
Throughout the spacious barn and kitchen *floor*,
At eve.

        There then the guests all seated down,
From every cottage home in all the town;
Some *old*, some *young*, and some quite *lately* born,
Vie with each other husking out the corn;
In social *chat* and merry *song* they *keep*
The golden ears fast flying from the heap;
While startled oft, the seated crowd appear,
At lucky swains, who find a crimsoned ear;
For in *such* luck, 'tis never deemed amiss,
To "go the round" and give the maids a kiss.
The sprightly boys, with bending baskets borne,
Remove the husks, and bear away the corn.

Then comes the hour that gathers large supplies
Of apple-dowdies [26] and of pumpkin-pies,
Then bends the board with viands, fruit, and wine; —
All hail! that gleeful hour, the olden time.
Then when the week hath turned its toil away
How mild and silent is the Sabbath-day!

The modest maiden churchward as she goes,
Proud in good looks and go-to-meeting clothes,
Across the glen untouched of dust or dews,
Bears in her hand her nice embroidered shoes;
Her stockings, too, home knit, of purest white; —
Now near the temple, pulls them on aright;
Then in the precinct of that holy place,
Where *loud* the parson grave dispenses grace,
Shines forth a *beauty flounced;* there seated down
The belle of all the beaux in Dracut Town.

THE MERRIMAC.

Such neat conceptions and such care in dress,
Deliberate judgments do not count the less.
Go back and see! A glance shall well suffice;
Our kind old mothers were the best of wives;—
They formed our habits, shaped our very lives;
Their precepts prayerful, pointed to the skies,
True joys most dear to early days alone,
Ungrudged they sought, forgetful of their own.
Men of my age! We hail that highland glee
That cheered the homes, the hearts of you and me
Of yore.   Ye matrons, too, whose childhood prime
Is merged in *memories* of the olden time,
Call up that hour! and bear me witness, too,
Of what in early life you used to do,—
How then on tip-toe cotton yarn you spun,
How buzzed the band and how the spindle run,
How moved the thread around the handy *reel,*

THE MERRIMAC.

How dear old mother whirled the linen wheel;
While at her knee the prattling baby stands
Provoking grandma with his little hands,
To feel the forkèd distaff's flaxy curl,
Or ferret out the curious whiz and whirl
Of wheel and spool; — heedless of *frown* or *fliers*
Or flax-comb keen. So fondly he admires.

Th' enchanting scenes of childhood's joyful day
We cherish still, though fled like flowers of May.
In truth, *alike* the habits had of yore,
That linen wheel and loom are known no more.

Anon advance the riper years of art,
In which inventions take decisive part,
Whence generous genius prosecutes the plan
To overcome the drudgery of man;
Makes *lifeless* things, impelled at his control,

THE MERRIMAC.

To do the duty of a living soul.
Hence cotton-gins and spinning-jennies fine
Outrun the wooden wheels of olden time.
Hence power of steam, applied on sea and land,
Expelling labor with a heavy hand,
Work startling wonders, through mechanic skill,
To move the car, the steamboat, or the mill.

By industry that artful LOWELL[27] led,
By faith far-seeing which a JACKSON[28] had,
The noisy flood, that o'er the breaker swells,
Is turned aside to follow huge canals.
Structures gigantic rise in prospect fair;
Cities that spread in beauty, here and there
Adorn the valley. Manufactories filled
With prompt machinery, as art had willed
Her *work*, in stately ranks now line the shore
Of Merrimac.

THE MERRIMAC.

Now changed that torrent roar!
Her fountains turned flow down in tranquil stream,
And rolling round the graded hills, between,
Through deep-laid channels, never washed before,
Propel the ponderous *wheel* with *mighty* power; —

The *wheels* " within *the wheel,*" with one consent,
Fly round and round, each on its duty sent;
Ten thousand spindles in their places spin,
Ten thousand spools fast wind their fibres in,
Ten thousand shuttles shoot across the web
Fed by the mules[29] slow back and forward led; —
Fast roll the fabrics from the rolling beam,
Complete in beauty, true in thread or seam;
The sheeting white, the listed broadcloths fine,
Neat satinet, and carpets superfine;
The gaudy prints and blankets plainer made,
For realms remote, for home or foreign trade.

THE MERRIMAC.

Workshops with throngs the villes environ,
Magic in power o'er wood, o'er steel and iron;
Alive in thought, and helping one another,
Onward in handy art advancing further,
Embracing all the works that man can do,
Through labor fruitful and inventions new.

The iron horse comes next to greet the day,
A gift of Stephenson. Now on the way,
With charioteer half hid upon his back,
Along where Merrimac had led the track
Bears high his head. *Held harnessed* to a train,
Fraught full of life, his energies aflame
Loud whistling wild, and fierce impelled *amain*,
He skirts the hills and snorts along the plain;—

When in the shades of night you chance to hear
The screaming whistle of that charioteer

THE MERRIMAC.

Afar; — then note the belching smoke and *fire;*
The train, impelled as if by Pluto's *ire,*
Darts like a dragon, *whizzing, winding* past,
As if from gates of hell let loose at last; —
Yet takes a charge to distant realms afar,
And brings a kind return in peace or war,
Shortens forever the tedious length of space,
Burdens to bear for every clime and race.

Not less the Telegraph, contrived of Morse,
Makes labor less. Thrown out upon its course
Full fraught with messages diffuses light,
Nor time nor space is measured in its flight, —
From State to State in every region hurled,
Skirting the ocean-bed from world to world
To bear the news; — to tender useful aid
To all the traffic of a foreign trade; —
To catch the culprit in his wayward flight,

THE MERRIMAC.

And turn him back to common law and right.
'Tis thus that "letters to the lightnings" given,
Flashed o'er the earth, reflect the light of heaven,
Make common cause for *good*, with all mankind.
So man progresses in the march of mind.

Nor less the fields in cultivation fine,
Through deep discovery in progressive time,
Advance. The patent plough, the scythe for mowing
And all things else of art, that seem worth knowing,
Invented now o'ercome the farmer's toil,
And make him monarch of this ancient soil.

Old PENNAKOOK puts on a modern name;
WAMESIT wild still onward does the same;
While AMOSKEAG, no more the red man's pride,
Makes MANCHESTER a city by her side.

THE MERRIMAC.

Southward and seaward, ancient NEWBURYPORT,
Of ships productive, strong in force and fort,
With even hand fulfils a noble part
In foreign commerce and the works of art.

Lowell is queen; — her history recalls
The might and memories of Pawtucket Falls.
Where Wonalancet *dwelt* in wigwam fair,
Now dwells, in pride of mansion, DR. AYER,
Whose nostrums pure and scientific skill,
To cure the nations from a tide of ill,
In doses daily measured by the tons,
And cords of calendars in numerous tongues,
Go forth. Here progress made in modern time,
Where science, art, and enterprise combine,
Tends but to tell how moves the world *apace*
At will and wisdom of the Saxon race.

THE MERRIMAC.

LAWRENCE and NASHUA, the later growth
Of cities chartered, proud in art and worth,
Still thrive. Wide interspersed are town and ville
At work in agriculture, shop, and mill;
HOOKSETT and SUNCOOK, once an Indian home,
With ancient Salisbury, drive the busy loom.

Pembroke and Bradford! Institutions *there*
Inspire the young in light of learning fair.
Here, too, old Andover, in science grand,
Gives gospel truth, glad-tidings to the land,
And Tyngsboro', Chelmsford! wander where you will,
The church and school are found, triumphant still.

Northward is Franklin, where *wild* waters meet
From mountain height and limpid lake to greet
Our Merrimac;—the rustic region *where*

THE MERRIMAC.

The noble WEBSTER[30] lived, — *first breathed* the air;
Schooled here in youth, in manhood he became
A nation's boast, a statesman known to fame;
A fame still chanted from the mountain rills,
Soft whispered wild in these his native hills.
That name *renowned* shall live *fore'er to be*
Revered with WHITEFIELD, slumbering near the sea.

Alike shall Pilgrims inspiration draw
At thought of PARSONS,[31] "Giant of the law;"
Whose life and learning found in book or plea,
Learned by the learned extend beyond the sea; —
His native NEWBURY strives in vain, alone,
Against the world to hold him as her own.

Here's AMESBURY, too, far seen in learnèd lights,
'Tis here a Whittier sings for *human rights*,
Whose prayerful cadence, high is heard in heaven

THE MERRIMAC.

Till God's full answer back to earth is given
In favor kind; — and yet through judgments just,
We're taught in wisdom, and in whom to trust.

Thus true it is, yet dread in deep disgrace—
An oligarchy of a southern race,
Born there of hell, and bred in slavery's school,
"Let loose their dogs of war" and sought to rule,
And Sumpter falls. "To arms!" the patriot cries;—
To arms *provoked*, the northern legions *rise;* —
Nor age, nor caste, nor different race, decline;
Alike in zeal, alike in faith *combine*
In manly strength. From all the vales and hills,
Out from mechanic shops, from *noisy* mills;
Physicians even, divines, and legal bar
Turn heroes brave and rally for the war;—

As when a bull disturbs a native hive,

THE MERRIMAC.

The bees ten thousand buzz and outward drive,
Black in the air the vast battalions bring
Their horrid weapons down, fierce on the wing,
Upon the herd. So bent on war, *alive*
Legions of Yankees from the northern hive
Leap forth aflame, in native strength and power,
Wielding dread engines yet unknown to war; —
Countless in cost, the preparation grand,
For deadly conflicts on the sea or land;
The monitor, in iron mail afloat; —
The monstrous mortar with a yawning throat; —
Vast shells and *shot within*, of strange invention; —
Six hundred pounders, slugs of huge dimension,
The new capt-rifle keen, the seven-shooter,
Ten thousand tons of iron, lead, or pewter.

 Armed thus the cohorts tramp the trembling plain,

THE MERRIMAC.

And crowd the mighty ships that plough the main,
The conscious thunders, muttering from afar,
Bemoan the horrors of impending war.
Not less the bolt, oft breaking from the sky,
Bespeaks dread vengeance, *threatened* from on high.
Four years of *darkness* curtains all the plain,
Four years of *conflict* on the land and main,
Earth deep in sorrow for the thousands slain,
Prove but the fruit, the penalty, and pain
Of sin. Yet high o'er all that earth betides,
Th' eternal Jove in majesty presides;
And in His mercy, sovereign will, and power,
Forgives the crime and turns the tide of war.
Now tumbling from her bulwarks, treason falls;
Loud ring the batteries, crushing in her walls,
The sweeping navies press the rebel shore,
From field to field the belching mortars roar.
Yet doth dread carnage *cease* at Heaven's will;

THE MERRIMAC.

The curse [32] is but removed, and all is still.
Great God of armies, we adore thy name
For thy forgiveness of a *nation's* shame,
Who, through the sea "led Israel like a flock,"
Hath led this modern Israel to "the rock
Beyond the flood." Oh, let us learn thee still;
Who bears thy image must obey thy will!
To whom but man should noble deeds belong,
To learn the right divine, to *spurn* the *wrong?*
What we would have of *others, do to them,*
Alike the work of nations as of men.

Of God-like man! — if thus he e'er appears,
'Tis when his truth outlives declining years,
Who ventures all in strength of youth or age,
In deeds divine his energies engage,
Who with one hand sustains a falling brother,
Yet grasps his country's flag firm in the other;

THE MERRIMAC.

To flaunt its folds on freedom's towering height,
In life's last hour still battles for the right;
'Tis such whose hand hath broken the galling fetter,
'Tis he whose life hath left the world the better,
To him shall rise a fervid, loud acclaim;
So beats a *nation's* heart at LINCOLN's *name;*
By whose true teachings treason lost its sway; —
Then passed the good man from the world away.
Still *Johnson* lives, — a GRANT to lead the van,
A *Sherman* bold, — a gallant *Sheridan.*
Hence shall the nation social pride maintain,
In sovereign States shall sovereign order reign.
Hail glorious day! 'Tis wisdom's plan ordained,
Above the *storm* is liberty proclaimed;
The sun of peace resplendent shines again;
O'er all the vale, it cheers th' abodes of men.

Come back, TISQUANTUM! if above ye dwell,

THE MERRIMAC.

Behold thy Merrimac, once loved so well;
Thy race had traced it from creation's start;
The white man turns it to the works of art;
Survey its progress *these three hundred* years,
Since up and down ye wandered here in tears
Alone, bereaved.

                Call once again to *view*
Thy thick-set forest *wild,* thy birch canoe,
Where now thy kindred sleep as from the first,
Where Pilgrim saints since mingled in the dust,
Where now the ploughman trudges in his toil,
Thoughtless of what *still lies* beneath the soil;
Oh! let us *know* from what thy name inspires, —
What is man's destiny, what Heaven *requires*
More *fully* still. From realms *eternal, fair,*
Tell us of hunting-ground, of glory *there,*
Where blissful prospect *Heaven* shall fulfill,
To generations *onward, upward still,* —

THE MERRIMAC.

While *purest* fountains flowing *failing never*
Shall swell the tide of *Merrimac* forever,—
Sure sign here given of God's enduring care,
For what we see in *heaven*, in *earth*, or *air*.

Boston: Printed by Innes and Niles, 37 Cornhill.

APPENDIX.

[1] THE "MERRIMAC" takes its rise in the White Mountains; is formed by the junction of the Pemigewaset and Winnipisseogee Rivers; is 110 miles long, and empties into the ocean near Newburyport. It has been said, "No river in the world *works* so hard as the Merrimac."

[2] SIR FRANCIS DRAKE visited New England in 1585.

[3] The Pilgrims landed Dec. 22, 1620.

[4] The *Indian's* mode of greeting was by a kiss.

[5] The Treaty with KING MASSASOIT was made March 22, 1621.

[6] Smoking was called *drinking* by the natives.

[7] TISQUANTUM, alias SQUANTO, died in Dec., 1622.

[8] Cattle were first brought into New England in 1624.

[9] MASSASOIT died, and PHILIP became king in 1670.

[10] SASSAMON was murdered Jan. 29, 1674, O. S. Two of the murderers, Tobias and Mattashinnamy, were executed June 8, 1674; the other, Wampapaquam, was shot in jail. The indictment against them contained the following count: —

"*For that being accused, that they did with joynt consent vpon the 29 of January anno 1674 att a place called Assowamset pond wilfully*

APPENDIX.

and of sett purpose and of malice fore thought and by force and armes murder John Sassamon another indian, by laying violent hands on him and striking him, or twisting his necke, vntil hee was dead; and to hyde and conceale this theire said murder att the tyme and place aforesaid did cast his dead body through a hole of the ice into the said pond."

[11] PHILIP was slain August 12, 1676.

[12] WONALANCET, a son of Passaconaway, lived at Pawtucket Falls, and was Chief in the Merrimac Valley from 1660 to 1677.

[13] PENNAKOOK is now *Concord, N. H.*

[14] WAMESIT is Lowell, and was called the Great Neck.

[15] KING WILLIAM'S war commenced in 1690 and ended in 1698.

[16] COTTON MATHER, a clergyman, born Feb. 12, 1662, and died Feb. 13, 1727, aged sixty-five.

[17] HANNAH DUSTIN and Mary Neff were taken captives at Haverhill, Mass., March 15, 1697. Assisted by Samuel Leonardson, they slew their captors on the 31st day of the same month. There were eight children in the Dustin family. When Mrs. D. was taken, the infant was slain against a tree. The other children escaped by flight, assisted by the father.

[18] MARY NEFF, the maid of Mrs. D., who, when the Dustin house was set on fire, chose captivity rather than to forsake her mistress and the infant.

[19] SAMUEL LEONARDSON was a boy who had been captured by the Indians prior to their attack upon the Dustin house, who, with Mary Neff, assisted Mrs. D. in killing the Indians on the island in the Contoocook.

APPENDIX.

[20] *Nashua*, a river emptying into the Merrimac from the west at Nashua, N. H.

[21] QUEEN ANNE's war of eleven years ended March 31, 1713.

[22] The *French* and *Indian* war of seven years ended May 18, 1763.

[23] The *Revolution* of seven years ended by definitive treaty Sept. 30, 1783.

[24] BENJ. PIERCE, a native of Chelmsford, Mass., was a captain in the Revolution, and was two years governor of New Hampshire, and died at Hillsboro' in 1839, aged eighty-one.

[25] JOHN STARK, a major-general in the Revolution, was a native of Londonderry, N. H., and died at Manchester May 8, 1822, aged ninety-four. He rests on the second bank of the Merrimac, in that city. At Bennington, on rallying his men he is reported to have said, "*We will gain the battle, or Molly Stark shall be a widow to-night.*"

[26] *Apple-dowdy*, a huge pie, which was common in the rural districts, and known by that name.

[27] FRANCIS C. LOWELL was a native of Newburyport. He died in 1817, aged thirty-eight. From him the city of Lowell took its name.

[28] PATRICK T. JACKSON was a native of Newburyport. He died Sept. 24, 1847, aged sixty-seven.

[29] *Mule*, an instrument for spinning thread for the web, worked by hand; called also *mule-jenny*.

[30] DANIEL WEBSTER, a native of Salisbury, now Franklin, N. H., died at Marshfield, Mass., Oct. 24, 1852, aged seventy.

[31] THEOPHILUS PARSONS, a native of the Parish of Byfield in New-

APPENDIX.

bury, Mass., was Chief-Justice of Massachusetts seven years, and died at Boston Oct. 30, 1813, aged sixty-four.

[32] The Rebellion commenced April 12, 1861, at the storming of Fort Sumpter, and ended at the surrender of *Lee*, April 9, 1865.

NOTE.— For an extended view of what is related in the context, the reader is referred to the following interesting works: Drake's History of the Indians, Bouton's History of Concord, Potter's History of Manchester, Fox's History of Dunstable, Cowley's History of Lowell, and Smith's History of Newburyport.

Boston: Printed by Innes and Niles, 37 Cornhill.

www.ingramcontent.com/pod-product-compliance
Lightning Source LLC
Chambersburg PA
CBHW030313170426
43202CB00009B/987